Street plan of Ilford pre-1914.

Bygone

ILFORD

The Clock Tower stood in the heart of Ilford from 1901 until 1923 when it was removed to South Park.

Bygone
ILFORD

Brian Evans

Phillimore

1989

Published by
PHILLIMORE & CO. LTD.,
Shopwyke Hall, Chichester, Sussex

ISBN 0 85033 707 0

Printed and bound in Great Britain by
BIDDLES LTD.,
Guildford, Surrey

To Susan

List of Illustrations

Frontispiece: Ilford's Clock Tower

Acknowledgements

Although I have tried to rely on information in my own collection, I would like to thank the following for their assistance: Mr. H. H. Lockwood; the London Borough of Redbridge Local Studies Library, particularly Peter Wright and Ian Dowling; Susan Curtis and Mrs. Jill Williams of the Valence House Museum and Reference Library. I am also grateful to the following for permission to reproduce illustrations: D. W. Clark; Guildhall Library, Department of Prints; P. Hotchin; the London Borough of Redbridge Local Studies Department; Science Museum. I apologise for any omission in these acknowledgements.

Preface

A Country Ramble from Cranbrook Road in 1910

The following walk was one of 26 published in a book four years before the outbreak of the First World War. Sadly, such rural peace was never to return. In the preface, the author comments:

> To some, perhaps, a few of the places mentioned may, at first sight, seem somewhat distant but by using the town's tramway system where possible, long walks through uninteresting streets may be avoided and the open country can be entered immediately on arrival at any of the termini; several of the distances have, in fact, been calculated from these termini.

Even so, this first walk starts in the very heart of the town, up a busy shopping street, yet still plunges into the green footpaths just beyond, a total of five or six miles.

> Few walks in Ilford afford more pleasure than that along the Cranbrook Road, from its commencement at Ilford Station to its termination at Fullwell Hatch, Barkingside – a distance of 3 miles. The road is usually in good condition, and its air is at times decidedly bracing and invigorating beyond the town. The business end has, of course, lost its country-like aspect, but something of its former beauty can be seen in the splendid chestnut and other trees which still, happily, remain in the gardens of the private houses. At the Wash is the little porter's lodge which stood behind the gates of old Cranbrook Hall. Many still living in Ilford can remember when there were only about half-a-dozen houses between the station and 'Valentines'. After passing the gates of the latter at the beginning of Emerson Road on the new Garden Suburb Estate, and the entrance to the public park beyond, the road has fields on either side of it. The little wooded dell on the right is all that remains of Sparks Wood, which is marked on a map dated 1774 as being on both sides of the road. The white house a little further along on the left is Gants Hill Cottage. Opposite is Cocklease Lane. Then comes the Horseshoes hamlet at the end of which is Little Gearies and the farm road and public path past Gaysham Hall. From here to Dr. Barnardo's Homes the road is very pretty and shady. Just past Great Gearies, with its cedar is Barkingside Recreation Ground (12 acres), purchased in 1899; it was formerly part of Gaysham Hall farm and provided a much needed playground for the district. (A few yards further on is the tram terminus.)
> Entering the gate, strike across the grass towards Holy Trinity Church and the Schools. The former was built in 1841 and contains a few modern stained glass windows; the tower was rebuilt only a few years ago. Opposite the church is the Vicarage. At the top of the road turn to the left along the farm road to Gaysham Hall (to the right leads to Claybury fence path and Tomswood Hill). At the end of the farm road the field path (or road) on the left takes back to Little Gearies in the Cranbrook Road, so follow the path to the right, which leads by the kitchen garden and lawn of the farm. The house, which is about 500 years old, contains some fine oak from Hainault Forest, and looks very picturesque with its white front and red roof. Here the path turns to the left along a hedge and through a 'kissing gate', past a cottage, round the corner to the right to another cottage (both belonging to Hedgeman's Farm), to the road leading to the farmhouse. Turn to the left down the road, opposite the end of which is Redbridge Lane with its smithy at the corner. The intersecting road leads to Beehive on the left and to St Swithin's farm and Woodford Bridge on the right. A little way down Redbridge Lane on the left, is a short field path leading to Beehive hamlet (Silver Street), and about five minutes beyond that is the field path, on the left, leading to the Castle and The Drive, which can now be followed.

Introduction

Origins

The heart of Ilford is only seven miles from London, on a slight rise on the east bank of the River Roding, just within the western boundary of the area known as Great Ilford, and in two thousand years this small rural settlement has grown into the important town of today.

In medieval times, different sections of the Roding carried their own special names, complementing the varied terrains through which the river flowed. In 1062, in the Woodford area, north of Ilford, it was called the Angrices Burne (grassland stream). Near Shellow, further north, it was known as the Sceolh (winding river), derived from an Old English word meaning awry. Ilford got its own name from the river – the Hile (c.958) or Hyle (c.1250), meaning 'the trickling Brook'. In ancient times, a ford was made here; the narrow predecessor of the present wide bridge, replaced in 1904, still displayed a slip of beach at its north eastern end where the ford had once been.

Nearby, sections of an ancient river bed have since been excavated and have produced a wealth of fascinating discoveries. In 1880 a lecture was given by Henry Walker with the intriguing title 'A Day's Elephant Hunting in Essex'. He describes a Saturday afternoon's visit to the Ilford 'game preserves', the Ilford brickearth pits of the 19th century where the bones of numerous different species were being unearthed.

> Thus we reach the brink of one of the pits. We reach the lower terra firma by a course of wheelbarrow planks. At length we are all assembled, first to receive the instructions of our guides, and then to unearth what game we can for ourselves. It now begins to dawn on the uninitiated in our party that elephant hunting in Essex, in these modern days, is an underground sport – a recreation restricted to the subterranean world and no longer carried on in the open ...
>
> ... It might be misleading if we said we were standing in the bed of the ancient Thames. And yet these alluvial precincts of the Roding certainly lie within the great shallow trough of what we now call the Thames Valley – that incalculably old line of drainage which has seen so many and eventful changes in the physical geography of South-eastern England.
>
> ... A perpendicular face of the river-bed rises before us some seventeen feet in height. Running from left to right until they disappear in the unexcavated ground, and pass away beneath modern Ilford, are horizontal bands of different coloured earths. These successive layers of loam and sand and gravel represent successive changes in the sediments brought down by the old and now vanished river which once flowed over the spot. In fact, we have here a lesson as to *how land is made*.

In 1863, a perfect skull of the British mammoth (*Elephas primigenius*) was unearthed in the bright yellow sand of the river bed. It was discovered by workmen about fifteen feet below the surface. The cranium was nearly entire, and only the upper portion of the left side had been slightly damaged by a workman's spade or pick. The tusk of the mammoth measured eight feet and eight inches. Remains of the fleece-clad rhinoceros, the great fossil ox and numerous freshwater shells were also found.

Other animal remains found at Ilford include three types of rhinoceros, the southern elephant, great hippopotamus, wild horse, Irish elk, stag, bison, brown and grizzly bears, wolf, fox, lion, beaver and water rat. The reason given by Walker for the existence of both warm and cold climate species in Britain during this unique period was the double circumstance of a retreating ice age and a rising of the land mass. England was originally joined to the Continent across what is now the North Sea and the English Channel. This

In 1812, while digging for brick-earth, in a field about 300 yards from the river Rodon, and 2 miles north of the Thames, some fossil remains were discovered. This field is part of an estate called Clements, situated on the left side of the road, leading from Ilford to Barking, belonging to John Thompson, esq.

The first stratum consists of two feet of black mould; the second, from 2 to 4 feet gravel; the third is red clay, from 8 to 10 feet; the fourth is sand, from 6 to 8 feet, in which are found different shells; at the bottom of this stratum lie the remains of various animals, in the circumference of 10 or 12 yards; as, the bones of oxen of a very large size; the horns and bones of stags; also, a spiral horn, which, on attempting to remove it, broke in pieces: this being measured, as it lay, was found to be nine inches in diameter, and, following the windings, 13 feet 4 inches in length. Besides these, an animal's head, (supposed to be that of a small deer, or goat,) which Sir Joseph Banks, President of the Royal Society, after examining the other remains, took to ascertain the species: and also the head bones and teeth of an elephant; one of the grinders in good preservation, with a fine enamel on it, measures near 9 inches in length, $3\frac{1}{4}$ in breadth, and weighs ten pounds. These fossil teeth do not resemble the living species either of Asiatic or African elephants. There are two species of fossil remains, which are known by the thinness and number of the plates on the triturating surface

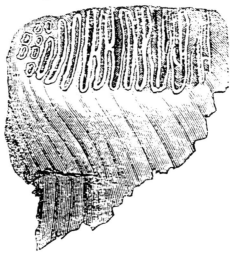

1. The brickfields of Ilford were the 'hunting ground' for those seeking fossilised animals during most of the 19th century. More recently, during reconstruction work in Richmond Road in 1984, further finds were carefully recorded by the Passmore Edwards Museum.

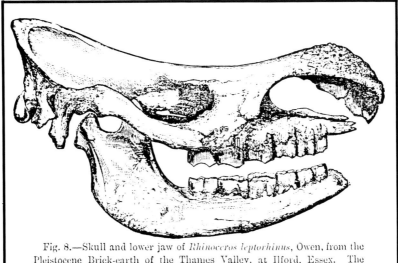

Fig. 8.—Skull and lower jaw of *Rhinoceros leptorhinus*, Owen, from the Pleistocene Brick-earth of the Thames Valley, at Ilford, Essex. The original, from the collection of the late Sir Antonio Brady, F.G.S., is now in the British Museum. See Geol. Mag. 1874. Decade II., vol. i., p. 398, pl. xv. [This woodcut is obligingly lent by Messrs. Cassell & Co., from their 'Natural History,' vol. ii., p. 334.]

2. The skull and lower jaw of a Rhinoceros. Other fossils discovered in Ilford included the mammoth, brown and grizzly bear, wolf, lion, beaver, wild horse and bison.

land mass stretched as far as Africa, leading to ideal conditions for animal migration. Vegetation had gradually returned after the Ice Age and alternations of climate encouraged both northern and southern species to wander over vast tracts of land, visiting the extreme limits of their climatic range.

Evidence of human occupation has been found at the Uphall location, next to the fossil animals. The site, known as Uphall Camp, was an earthwork on the western side of Ilford Lane, just north of the Barking boundary. In the 19th century, it was thought to show signs of the existence of early man but no careful excavation was made and Howard's chemical factory was built on the site. Recently the land became available again for excavation and pottery from a Middle Iron Age settlement of the 2nd century B.C. was found. Also discovered, to the east of the Roding, were round houses, some with porches and agricultural stores of a similar shape, as well as other buildings, pointing to a thriving settlement of this period. Boundary and enclosure ditches surrounded the settlement which was still active in the next century.

The crossroads at Ilford are connected with the Celtic presence in the district. Ancient green paths met here – Ley Street, Barking (now Ilford) Lane, Green Lane (which, until it was diverted in the 19th century further east into the High Road, once continued west into Barking Lane) and Back Lane (or Roden Street). It is quite possible that these green ways led to holy places connected with Druidic or pre-Christian religion. Such sites often continued into Christian worship. Green Lane, for instance, ran eastwards to Hornchurch where the Priory of St Bernard later stood on its little hill (now St Andrew's church). The adjacent hospital site has always been contained in a curious island of ground and a path on its far side may have been part of the ancient paths system. The junction of paths took

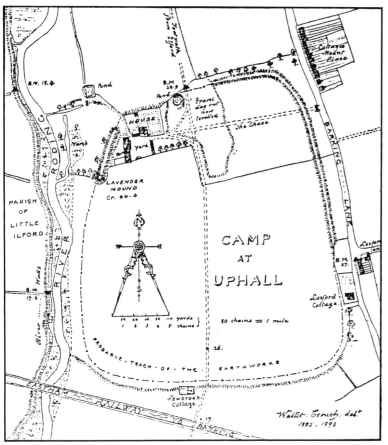

3. Plan of Uphall Camp, a fort of 48 acres, before its exploration was halted by factory development. Recently it became available again for exploration and, although it had been damaged by building, there have been further interesting discoveries. The site has revealed evidence of human occupation from the Middle Iron Age.

4. Lavender Mount – an artificial mound added on to what was already higher ground on the east bank of the Roding. The name derives from a former owner of the land but the origins of the mound are obscure. Recent excavations on this Uphall site have revealed a Roman military building as well as evidence of the Iron Age inhabitants.

the appearance of a wheel or fyflot symbol which may have some significance.

Several attempts have been made to explain the etymology of the placenames Seven Kings and Chadwell, to the east. Seven Kings has been enshrined in local legend as the meeting place for that number of Saxon rulers. Reaney prefers 'Seofecingas' – the settlement of the people of Seofeca. Yet number symbolism has the powerful ability to survive from a distant magical past. Bayley in *Archaic England* explains the widespread impact on placenames of descriptions referring to the multiple facets of the Druidic God:

> There is little doubt that Honor Oak, Gospel Oak, Sevenoaks etc. derived their names from oaks once sacred to the Uch or High, the Allon or Alone, who was alternatively the *Seven Kings* or Three Kings.

This theory gains strength from the proximity of Chadwell. St Chad (or Cedd) was supposed to have been an early Christian missionary who made many converts in Essex. There are several wells in Essex which are said to have been dedicated to him but even Reaney, the authority on placenames, comments that 'St. Chad's Well' is 'clearly a late hagiological invention'. Instead we might look to the 'Kaadman' of Celtic lore. Again Bayley says, 'In Irish cad means holy: good and cad are the same word ... The hawk a symbol of the Kaadman was the Uch or high flying bird which soared sun-wise and hovered overworld eying the below with penetrating and all seeing vision'. Thus Chadwell and Seven Kings may have been sacred to the Celts, their groves filled with the mystic incantations of Druidic ritual.

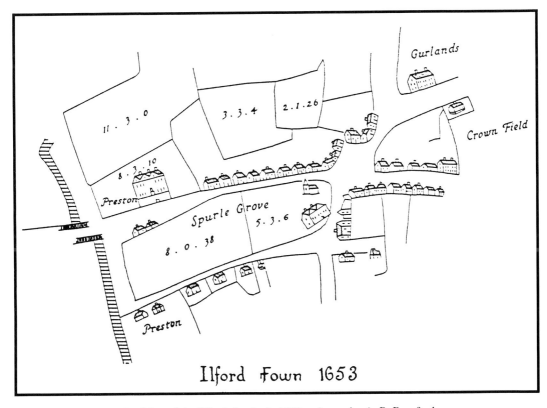

5. Map of the Ilford district in 1653 redrawn by A. B. Bamford.

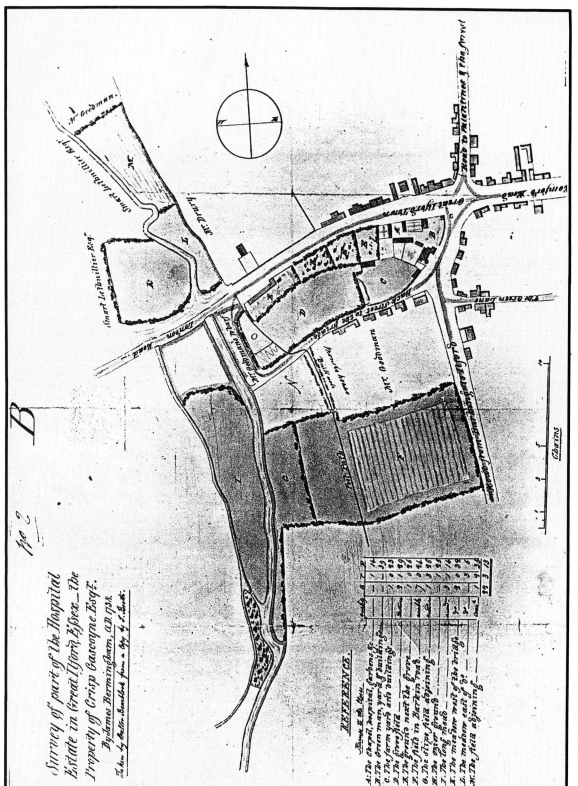

6. Bermingham Survey of Ilford's nucleus in 1738, showing the Hospital Island and a footpath as well as the original exit of Green Lane.

Cavalcade

In time the iron hand of Roman civilisation was felt by the islanders of early Britain and the Celtic inhabitants began to retreat. The Great Roman military road was laid across the wastes and groves of the Druids in Essex. It still remained a lonely, quiet backwater except when a procession of foot soldiers and military carts used the highway. The backcloth of heathland and forest would remain for many centuries to come, but other civilised features gradually began to appear on the landscape. Evidence of Roman villa homesteads in the hinterland of the Great Road increased. An important settlement is indicated from finds made at the gravel pits in the Carswell area of Barkingside. These finds included a considerable amount of pottery, with a mortarium rim impressed SOLLVS F., of the late 1st century. In 1909 a decorated Samian bowl was discovered on the Uphall site – this attractive, orange pottery is usually associated with a more luxurious standard of living than the coarser wares. When this site recently became available again for excavation, further work revealed a small military structure resembling a watchtower or signal station of the 3rd or 4th centuries. There is no evidence that man continued to live in this area during the following Dark Ages, but it is quite possible that Romano-British inhabitants survived amidst the ruins of the Roman era abandoned by the military.

Gradually these people were succeeded by new invaders from across the North Sea. The arrival of the Saxons led to the construction of an important abbey at Barking in about A.D. 666. The original foundation, created by St Ethelwald (soon to become Bishop of London) for his sister Ethelburga was almost certainly a dual one, for both monks and nuns. The event was a historic landmark for the little hamlet on the high road, beside the river crossing. Processions of travellers would now leave the main road here, as this was the only way to reach the abbey.

Ilford's progress received a setback when the Danes rampaged through eastern England and burnt the monastery to the ground in A.D. 870. It lay derelict for a century and may never have risen again to its later glory had not King Edgar the Peaceable suffered a fit of repentance over a previous wrong involving the church. Letheuillier, the local historian, believed that, during these rebuildings of the abbey, material from Roman remains at the Uphall site was plundered and incorporated into the abbey itself; some Roman tiles have been observed in the remaining abbey stonework. The abbey was rebuilt again in the 12th century when it reached the height of its influence and prosperity. Two of the reigning king's daughters were abbesses and it is also known that William the Conqueror and his troops over-wintered at Barking in January 1067. From the time of Edward the Confessor (1046-66) to that of Charles I, English sovereigns frequently travelled along the High Road at Ilford, on the way to the royal palace at Havering-atte-Bower. In November 1321, affairs of state were conducted from Ilford when, in a surprise move, Edward II marched against the Kentish and Essex rebels. The Close and Patent Rolls show that he stayed at Ilford for at least two days, conducting crown business. The town must have witnessed some impressive royal processions passing along the road. Some of these, such as Elizabeth I's, would have taken a considerable time to pass

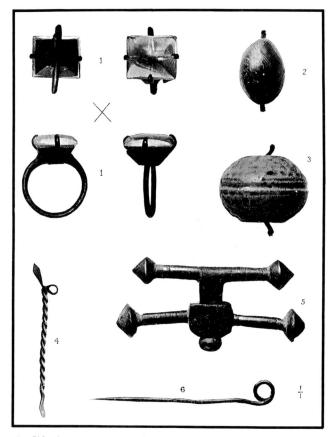

7. Ilford grew up to meet the needs of travellers passing through this crossroads hamlet en route to nearby Barking. These articles found at Barking belonged to medieval travellers. They include four views of an abbess's ring, an onyx bead, a spindle whorl or bead, a tooth-pick and ear-scoop combined, a small purse-swivel and a bronze pin.

through. It is known that King David of Scotland came to Ilford to visit his sister; when he arrived, he found her washing the feet of lepers.

With all this traffic on the Great Road, the threat of disease within such a small community was rife. With limited sanitation, infection could spread with terrifying speed. An attempt to combat this problem came with the founding of a Lazar House or Leper Hospital at the Ilford crossroads, by the Abbess of Barking during the reign of King Stephen, *c.*1140. Provision was made for 13 lepers, a prior, a master and other staff. Rules drawn up in 1346 by Ralph Stratford, Bishop of London, ordered that every leper should take an oath of chastity and obedience to the abbess upon his admission. Further along the Great Road, there was another hospital at Brook Street, near Brentwood. A small road ran alongside the Ilford hospital and there is still a by-road here called Spital Lane. During the Middle Ages, travellers would have stopped to offer up prayers in the hospital at the shrines of the Virgin Mary and St Thomas.

The Great Road was certainly a lively place and the presence of wealthy travellers attracted a certain criminal element. Some robberies would occur surreptitiously whilst travellers were resting. In other cases, there would be a more dramatic robbery along the highway. In the 1650s, one victim was a Rector of Hutton 'riding on the highway between Chadwell and Ilford' where he had a bag and £16 10s. stolen from him by 'a poulterer and two women'. Often, firearms were used and the result could be more serious. In December 1775, the *Norwich Mercury* newspaper reported that:

> On Monday morning, early, the Norwich coach was again stopped at the 6th milestone at Ilford by five footpads. An excise officer of this city, who was an outside passenger and had a brace of pistols discharged them both and killed one of the villains on the spot. The guard being unwilling to fire, the excise man took his carbine from him, fired it, and broke the legs of another, who is in custody.

The carbine had been developed for the cavalry and was often used by the coaching guards to protect the passengers and their valuables. Such casualties, however, did not deter others mounting similar attacks. A crime is recorded in the church register of St Edward's, Romford: 'Burials – 1794 Oct 14th; James Martin, a King's Messenger, shot near the Stoup by five footpads'. This crime took place on the highway adjacent to Stoup Lane (now Station Road, Goodmayes) and can be seen on the Turnpike Map. Some maps mark this point as 'King's Water Stoup', as it was a watering place for cattle on the way to the market at Romford.

8. Views of the interior and exterior of the Leper Hospital chapel in 1816.

The Hospital Chapel

Ilford, Essex

Interior View Looking West.

The Chapel From Dr Schimel's Garden.

9. A later sketch of the chapel in 1890.

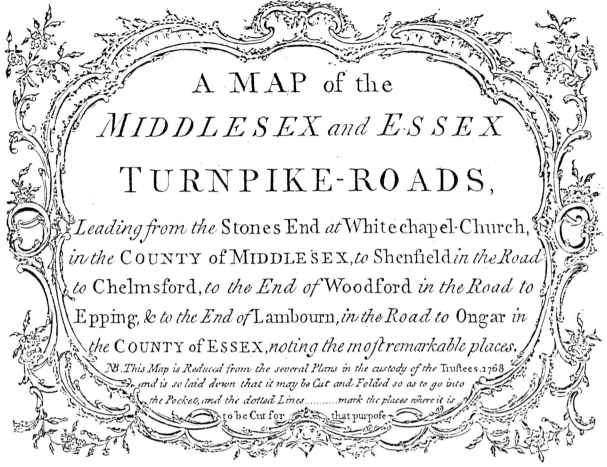

A MAP of the MIDDLESEX and ESSEX TURNPIKE-ROADS,

Leading from the Stones End at Whitechapel-Church, in the COUNTY of MIDDLESEX, to Shenfield in the Road to Chelmsford, to the End of Woodford in the Road to Epping, & to the End of Lambourn, in the Road to Ongar in the COUNTY of ESSEX, noting the most remarkable places.

NB. This Map is Reduced from the several Plans in the custody of the Trustees. 1768 and is so laid down that it may be Cut and Folded so as to go into the Pocket, and the dotted Lines............mark the places where it is to be Cut for that purpose

10 & 11. Extracts from a map of the Middlesex and Essex Turnpike Roads in 1768. This is the Great Road as the coach traveller knew it. Notice the name Cricklewood Bridge where Cricklefield athletic ground now stands.

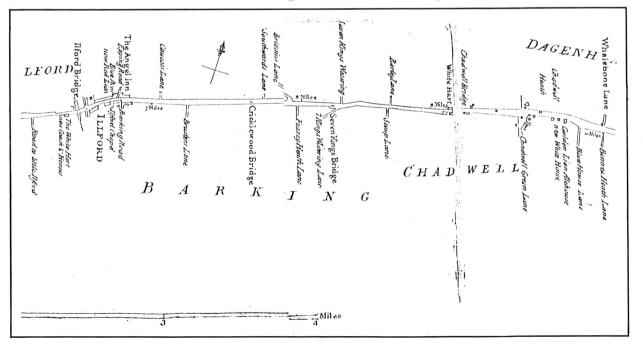

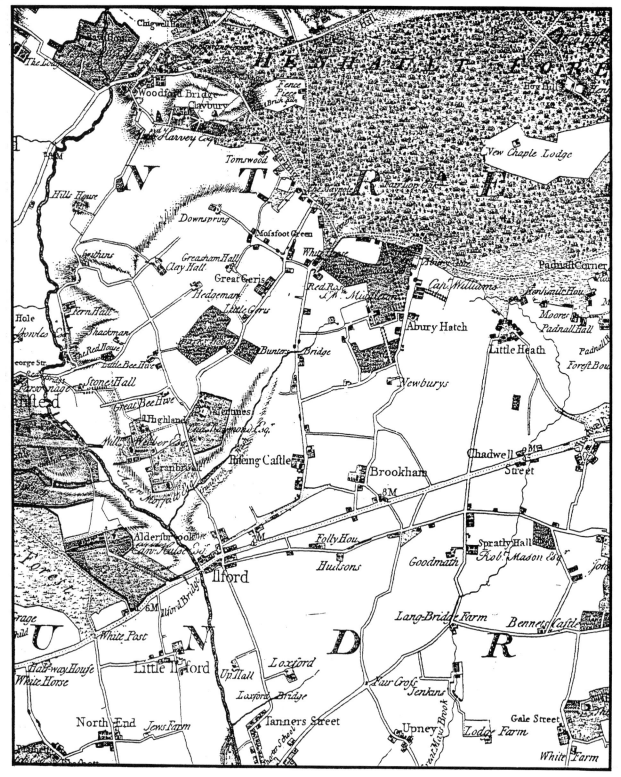

12. Chapman and André's Map of 1777 clearly shows the extent of the forest reaching into Ilford. The forest economy was important to the inhabitants of the Ilford district.

13. Barking town and its abbey. This engraving from a view by Prout in the early 19th century gives a strong impression of the great buildings that once existed in the town. The abbess was an individual with impressive political and financial clout in an age when the Church as an institution had great influence.

Ilford Bridge 1886.

Ilford Bridge 1906.

14. The old and new Ilford bridges. Every traveller had to cross the Roding over the various bridges that have stood here and the original ford which gave the place its name.

COMMERCIAL HOTEL & POSTING HOUSE.

15. *The Angel*, Ilford, was one of the travellers' hostelries and saw many of the comings and goings of the coaching age.

Breaking Away
A Century of Change

In the second half of the 18th century, Ilford was still only a small subsidiary of Barking parish. The old order of landowners and workers living in a settled community still existed. Within a few decades, however, as the 19th century dawned, there were signs of impending change. The traditional relationships were being undermined by the new commercial rich who were taking over most of the large houses. One of the first was Josiah Child who acquired Wanstead House and transformed it into a dazzling mansion. Professional and non-manual workers also began to appear in the community, to provide new services.

These newcomers challenged Ilford's dependence upon Barking. As far back as 1650, Jurors had come before the Commission on Essex Returns of the Parliamentary Inquisition into the true value of Livings and asked that the town of Great Ilford, with about 60 families, should be made a separate parish. Mention was also made of the number of families 'living in the Forest' in Great Ilford Ward, four or five miles away from Barking parish church. These same inhabitants of Ilford had already managed to obtain £40-£50 per annum from sequestered tithes belonging to the hospital, so that a sermon could be preached every Sunday in the Hospital church.

From about 1823, local churchmen and landowners lobbied for the construction of a new church. After 1825 this proposal hardened into a demand for a new civil and ecclesiastical parish. Robert Hall-Dare of Cranbrook, John Scrafton Thompson of Clements and a few others were prominent in this campaign. The battle for a civil parish was lost but a new ecclesiastical division was approved. Ilford was on its way to independence at last. A new parish church was built on land given by Thompson, at the east end of the High Road. The vicar, appointed in 1837, received $^4/_9$ of the ancient Barking vicarage tithes.

The trade generated from stage coaches passing along the Great Essex Road fuelled Ilford's prosperity. A new form of transport, however, was soon to arrive. Plans were made for a railway to be constructed from west to east, running along the entire width of the ward. Hundreds of construction navvies and workers camped by the spoil heaps or were billeted in nearby cottages and barns. The railway opened in 1839 and contributed to the subsequent growth in Ilford's population. The figures for Ilford ward rose from 1,724 in 1801 to 3,742 in 1841 (the figures for Chadwell ward rose from 317 to 758). Growth continued in the 1850s and, by 1881, the population had grown to 7.645. By now, Ilford was beginning to acquire more urban characteristics. Hainault Forest was savagely destroyed and farm estates were built on the land; the housing boom was about to start.

Ilford's civil separation from Barking in 1888 seems finally to have happened rather effortlessly. Barking's town fathers were probably uncomfortably aware of the growing complexity of Ilford's problems, including the provision of services to the burgeoning housing estates. Barking had its own problems of renewal which could be better faced without those arising from Ilford's accelerating growth.

16 & 17.   These old wooden cottages at the top of Ilford Lane were removed in order to widen the road for the trams and other traffic. Ilford Lane was originally known as Barking Lane, when Ilford was still a part of Barking parish.

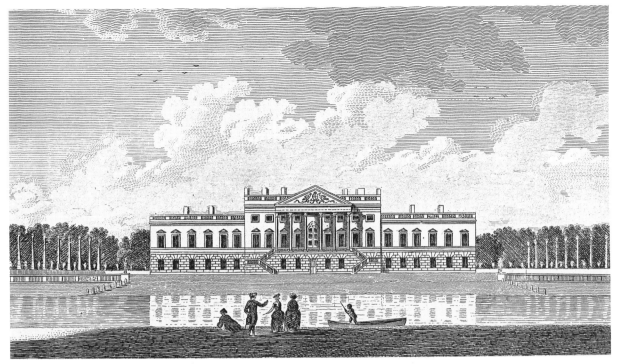

18. Wanstead House, just beyond Ilford, was one of the most magnificent Essex mansions. It was started in 1715 by Colen Campbell for Sir Richard Child, replacing an earlier house where Leicester entertained Elizabeth I. Its front extended for 260 feet and its gardens stretched for three quarters of a mile westwards from the house and half a mile eastwards.

19. Claybury Hall, engraved in 1806. It had been the residence of the famous Sir Christopher Hatton during the reign of James I.

20. Valentines, a typical Jacobean residence, was extensively rebuilt in 1811. It was originally built in the late 17th century by James Chadwick, son-in-law of John Tillotson (Archbishop of Canterbury). The archbishop must have spent many hours walking in the gardens, deep in religious thought. It has now become a public park and more than 100 acres are covered with attractive trees and plants.

21. Mrs. Ingleby, the last Lady of Valentines, was a benefactress and patron of many good causes in the locality.

22a. & b.   Two old wells – Ilford's original water supply. Many of the wells were supposed to have medicinal properties.

23.   The Castle was not an ancient fortification but was built in the grounds of Highlands as a mausoleum by Sir Charles Raymond in 1765. The actual building was triangular and there were vaults in the mound beneath. In the event it was never used for its intended purpose, merely serving as a picturesque landmark. It was finally demolished in 1923.

24. With the building of this church Ilford at last became a separate parish.

25. Ilford village in 1880.

Ilford's Rural Past

Even by the second half of the 19th century, Ilford was still predominantly a rural area. One Ilfordian, who came to the place as a young man in 1868, remembered how it seemed hundreds of miles away from the city instead of only seven, 'it was so quiet and peaceful'. George Gott, born at Mossford Green in 1850, said Ilford then was 'all sky and turnips'. In 1880, Henry Walker, on his fossil elephant hunt at the brickfields in Ilford Lane, describes the view:

> The landscape scenery, might we linger to enjoy it, would doubtless charm us with something of idyllic beauty. All around us the peaceful aborigines of Ilford pursue their wonted toil. Their life's employ would seem to be the cartage of manure. This staple industry of modern Ilford engrosses all the rural population. They stack the precious tilth in massive banks along the road, and seem to grudge the narrow embrasure in the long unlovely parapet that leads to many a cottage. Such are the charms of the Ilford country in June.

26.   Riotous assembly at Fairlop Fair – a satirical view by Thomas Tegg. Later views show respectable Victorian family groups picnicking, although there was usually a rowdier element.

27. Haymaking at Aldborough Hatch Farm before the First World War. The cart is very traditional although the workers are no longer wearing smocks.

Walker also mentions that brick-making was a two-season operation: 'In the Spring the ground is opened for the purpose of removing the earth which in the Autumn is to be made into bricks'. The brick pits were situated on the east side of Ilford Lane, on the west side below Uphall camp, and in the High Road.

The first inroad into the farmland was the breaking up of the Clements Estate in 1879. Road-building in Ilford started a building bonanza unparalleled elsewhere around London. One of the first developers to see Ilford's possibilities was A. Cameron Corbett who built the Clementswood Estate on part of the land, while Aaron Withers of Ilford Hall developed another large part of Clements. Other estates followed in quick succession – Ilford Lodge (1883), Birkbeck (1893), Grange (1894), Cranbrook, Loxford and Uphall (all c.1897), Mayfield and Downshall (1898). The last two, at Goodmayes and Seven Kings, were described as Klondyke Estates because like the gold prospectors' towns in that area of Canada the dwellings were built very quickly around a chaos of unmade roads and unfinished services. Many Britons were going out to try and make their fortunes in the Canadian goldfields so it was a topical reference everybody understood. Corbett soon ensured that new railway stations were built to serve the hundreds of houses which had sprung up. The railway had to provide for a huge increase in commuting traffic.

Fears about the speed of development resulted in a campaign for the council to acquire nearby parkland before it was built on. This led to the acquisition of the first part of Valentines Park, in the face of some shortsighted local opposition. This part, the furthest from the house which still remained as a private estate, was at first called Central Park. Despite continuing development, many acres of countryside and farmland still surrounded the built-up areas when war came in 1914.

28. Aldborough Hatch at the beginning of the century was still a self-contained rural community with medium-sized farms and a scattered population of approximately five hundred. *The Dick Turpin Inn*, down a short twisting lane north of the church, was a favourite haunt of cyclists on fine Sundays.

29. Tasker commented of St Peter's church, 'Many people have been puzzled to account for such a solid-looking church in so small a place, for it is not generally known that the stones of which it is composed at one time served as a bridge across the Thames at Westminster'. Apparently, the contractor for the church also built the new Westminster Bridge. He found it cheaper to use the stone removed from the 1750 bridge instead of using new bricks from the nearby Ilford brickyards.

30. Looking south from Fulwell Hatch towards the crossroads and Barkingside High Street. The place of refreshment was formerly a public house.

31. At the top end of Barkingside High Street, above what is now Freemantle Road, stood this group of buildings including the 'Cyclists' Rest'.

32. Goodmayes Farm, with its grazing horses, was an impressive old building standing among fields, with footpath walks all around it. It was located south of the development along Green Lane.

33. A footpath across the fields between Aldborough Road and Little Heath led to a spot called 'Happy Valley'. Here, a pretty wooded dell opened out onto a plank bridge across the Seven Kings Water and it was a favourite haunt of children.

34. These old gates at South Park Avenue contrast with the mature trees in the background. South Park was formed from 32 acres of the old Loxford Hall Estate, purchased in 1899 for £11,200. The water for a new lake was drawn from the Loxford Water as the historic Seven Kings Brook is here called.

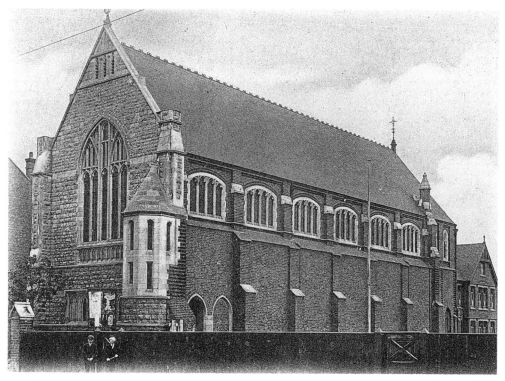

35.   A temporary iron building dedicated to St Peter and St Paul was blessed in 1895. A permanent church with the same dedication, shown here, was opened in June 1899 to hold 560 worshippers of the Roman Catholic faith.

36.   Because of building development in the Cranbrook area, more room was needed for worship in the St Clements district. A church hall dedicated to St Andrew was erected in 1906. A permanent church and a separate parish for this district had to wait until 1924.

37. (*above*) In a town of such sudden growth as Ilford, the churches played an important part in establishing community spirit and providing social facilities during the early days of development. The Baptist chapel, High Road, was built for £5,400 and was meant to seat five hundred. By 1900 the congregation had outgrown its accommodation and a new church was opened in Cranbrook Road.

38. (*above right*) One of the most successful churches and ministries in Ilford was that of the Congregational union and Henry Vine. This magnetic preacher built up the membership of his church from 110 in 1897 to 979 in 1927. His death in 1930 brought sadness to Ilfordians of all creeds. Such was his influence that the church was renamed the Vine Memorial church.

39. Another fine-looking minister, the Revd. Henry Davis Bull, issued this postcard of himself during his ministry at Goodmayes Congregational church.

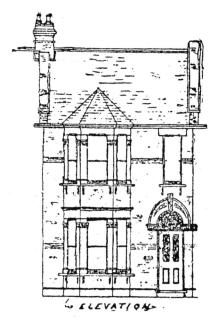

ᴸ ELEVATION .

These Superior VILLA RESIDENCES now being erected in Thorold-road, Ilford, by Messrs. Kydd, of Forest Gate.

They contain Three Bedrooms, Bathroom (h. and c.), Two Sitting Rooms, Kitchen, Scullery (h. and c.), Two W.C.'s, Coalhouse, &c.

They have a frontage of 18 feet, and long Forecourts and Gardens.

They are fitted with Electric Bells, Tiled Hearths, Chandeliers, Hall Lamp, &c.

The Roads and Paths are made and paved.

Rental value, £28 per annum. Lease 99 years. Ground Rent, £5 10s

Price £250 (if required only £30 need be paid down and the balance by instalments), or can be purchased Freehold, £410 each.

Apply at the Office on the Works, Thorold-road (within six minutes of Ilford Station).

---

40. An 1899 advertisement for superior villa residences in Thorold Road, with an estate agent's advertisement underneath.

41a & b. Two examples of Victorian houses in Ilford.

42. Councillor W. P. Griggs, who developed the Cranbrook Park Estate, was a large-scale property promoter, although not as big as Cameron Corbett.

43. On the left of this picture is the drive to W. P. Griggs' housing estate, with the Old Lodge originally at the entrance to Cranbrook Hall grounds. In the middle is the wash, a shallow area of water through which horses and carts would be driven in order to cool them down.

44. A second view of this area in summer with the trees obscuring the wash pond. The Cranbrook Park Estate notice can be clearly seen on the left. Today, Valentines telephone exchange has been built over the wash, but a culvert carrying the stream can still be seen in front. On the right is the entrance to Valentines Park, or Central Park as it was called at the time of this photograph.

45.   A view from further up the drive.

46.   Cranbrook Road shopping area looking south towards the station in those peaceful Edwardian days. A large churn sits awkwardly on the back of a milk float on the left. Jarvis's fruiterers and greengrocers is the second shop on the left. The trees in the background are in the grounds of Ilford cottage, still undeveloped.

47. Wellesley Road was one of the roads built between St Clements and the station.

48. As time went on, the northern part of the Cranbrook Road or Barkingside Lane area began to acquire suburban roads, although open farmland lay just beyond. Beattyville Gardens are shown here in the 1930s.

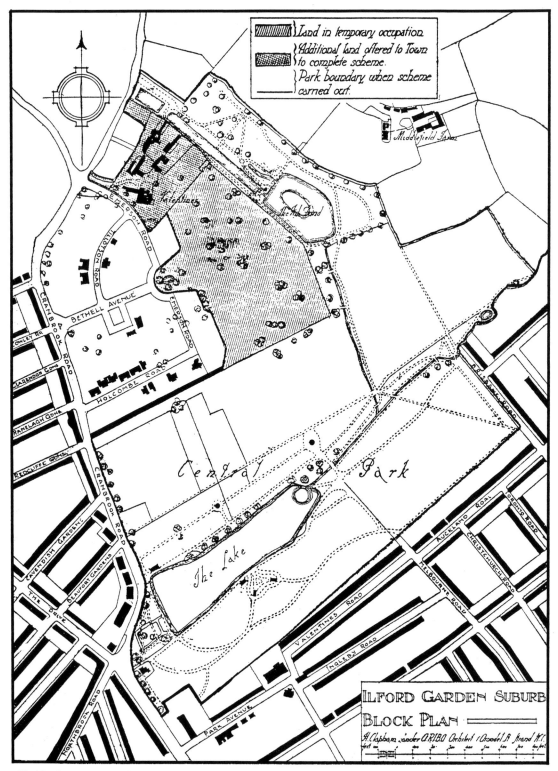

Land in temporary occupation.

Additional land offered to Town to complete scheme.

Park boundary when scheme carried out.

Middlefield Farm

The New Pond

Central Park

The Lake

ILFORD GARDEN SUBURB
BLOCK PLAN

H. Clapham Lander A.R.I.B.A. Architect / Oxendel R. Strand W.C.

49. As the open ground near the centre of Ilford began to be developed, a Committee was formed to campaign for the retention of the remaining Valentines House grounds before they too were sold. This campaign, which issued publicity around 1911 showing the land threatened, was successful in raising support and funds to add large areas to the existing Central Park.

50. A drawing of the Glade with the intended extension to the Park, 1911.

Transport Revolution

51. One of the last runs of the Fairlop 'Boat' at the very beginning of the 20th century. It represents the age of horse transport, although no stranger vehicle could be thought of. The view in the High Road includes the shops in the development known as Market Parade: John Lovibond, brewer and wine & spirit merchant, at no. 6; Cole & Deakin, ironmongers, at no. 5 and E. Langston, clothier, at no. 4.

THE EASTERN COUNTIES RAILWAY
IS NOW OPEN
FROM THE TEMPORARY STATION, DEVONSHIRE STREET, NEAR MILE END TURNPIKE, TO
ROMFORD.

PASSENGER TRAINS WILL START AS FOLLOWS:

FROM LONDON.
MORNING.
15 minutes to 10 o'Clock.
*15 minutes past 11 „

AFTERNOON.
15 minutes to 2 o'Clock.
15 minutes past 3 „
15 minutes past 5 „
15 minutes past 6 „
15 minutes to 8 „

FROM ROMFORD.
MORNING.
9 o'Clock.
30 minutes past 10 „
*12 „

AFTERNOON.
30 minutes past 2 o'Clock.
4 „
30 minutes past 5 „
7 „

LEAVING THE INTERMEDIATE STATIONS, VIZ:—

STRATFORD.

DOWN TRAINS.	UP TRAINS.
MORNING.	**MORNING.**
5 minutes to 10	23 minutes past 9
*25 minutes past 11	7 minutes to 11
AFTERNOON.	3 minutes past 12
5 minutes to 2	**AFTERNOON.**
25 minutes past 3	7 minutes to 3
5 minutes to 5	23 minutes past 4
25 minutes past 6	7 minutes to 6
5 minutes to 8	23 minutes past 7

ILFORD.

DOWN TRAINS.	UP TRAINS.
MORNING.	**MORNING.**
4 minutes past 10	14 minutes past 9
*26 minutes to 12	16 minutes to 11
	*14 minutes past 12
AFTERNOON.	**AFTERNOON.**
4 minutes past 2	16 minutes to 3
26 minutes to 4	14 minutes past 4
4 minutes past 5	16 minutes to 6
26 minutes to 7	14 minutes past 7
4 minutes past 8	

THE TRAINS WILL NOT RUN ON SUNDAY AT THE HOURS MARKED *

TABLE OF FARES.

	STRATFORD.			ILFORD.			ROMFORD.		
	1st Class.	2nd Class.	3rd Class.	1st Class.	2nd Class.	3rd Class.	1st Class.	2nd Class.	3rd Class.
LONDON.	6d.	6d.	6d.	1s. 6d.	1s.	9d.	2s. 6d.	1s. 6d.	1s.
STRATFORD.				1s.	9d.	6d.	2s.	1s. 6d.	1s.
ILFORD.							1s. 6d.	1s.	9d.

Passengers and Parcels may be Booked at all the above named Stations, at

**THE GLOUCESTER COFFEE-HOUSE, PICCADILLY;
BULL AND MOUTH, REGENT CIRCUS,
MOORE'S, OLD GREEN MAN AND STILL, 122, OXFORD STREET;
AND THE THREE NUNS, ALDGATE.**

Omnibuses conveying Passengers and Parcels to and from the Trains, call regularly at the above Offices, and Romford Coaches (in connexion with the Railway) run daily to and from Brentwood, Chelmsford, Hornchurch, Upminster, and Ockendon.

The Servants of the Company are strictly prohibited from receiving any Fee or Gratuity whatever.

ADELAIDE PLACE, LONDON BRIDGE,
August, 1839.

52. 'The Eastern Counties Railway is now open.' Although trials of the locomotives occurred beforehand, the official inauguration took place on 20 June 1839, the trains running from a temporary terminus at Mile End (Devonshire Street) to Romford.

53. 'View of the Ilford station.' On the opening day two trains were run in the same direction on parallel tracks. A splendid company was on board when the trains arrived at Ilford, announced by the firing of the cannon. The trackside was lined with crowds including ladies in fine dresses. The trains were brought to a stop but no one could alight as the station building was incomplete.

54. After opening the old Ilford station remained in use for many years, mostly unaltered. An interesting structure on the roof of the main building, on the far London side of the tracks, may have housed a bell. It is known that a bell was rung at Brentwood station in the early days to warn intending passengers of the approach of a train. The original platforms were raised only slightly above the track.

55. William Pallant, stationmaster at Ilford from about 1875, saw Ilford growing round the railway. The station grew too, from a wayside stopping place to a large commuter station. In 1876 there were 90 trains daily, in 1901 there were 450 daily trains in winter and 520 passing through in the summer. Extra capacity had to be found. The track was widened, additional rails were laid to Ilford and the suburban service was altered to end at Ilford instead of Forest Gate. The old station was pulled down and replaced by this new one spanning the bridge over the line, opened on 1 July 1894.

56. On 1 July 1898 two platforms were added on the express train side of the station, making five in total. The special entrance at the far London end of the platforms led directly to the Grange Estate. This was partly funded by Cameron Corbett to enable passengers in his properties quicker access to the station. This view looking towards the Broadway shows a watertank on the right, above the bay platform.

57. Fairlop station, as it appeared in the latter days of steam. On the right, at the end of the station wall, is a signal attached to a background board, making it more clearly visible to oncoming drivers.

58. No. 8508 heading the Continental Boat Express, seen here at Chadwell Heath. Local services were also flourishing. The areas north of Ilford were reached by a line from Stratford to Loughton via Snaresbrook, dating from 1856. In 1903 a new rail link from Ilford itself via Newbury Park, Barkingside, Hainault and Chigwell to Woodford was opened on 1 May. This joined up with the Loughton-Stratford branch, enabling an 'Ilford loop' service to be run in two directions.

59. The old Liverpool Street station, most of which has recently been demolished, was the goal of most Ilford commuters en route to their city jobs.

60. Tram no. 2 in pristine condition, outside the Ley Street depot in 1903. The town, never having had a horse tramway, launched straight into an electric version. It was inaugurated in a blaze of glory and a thunderstorm on the afternoon of Saturday 14 March 1903 from this depot.

61. Tram no. 15 on the Chadwell Heath run – there was not much protection for the driver in bad weather! On the inauguration run from the depot the three cars accelerated away from each other in the hands of their amateur (councillor) drivers.

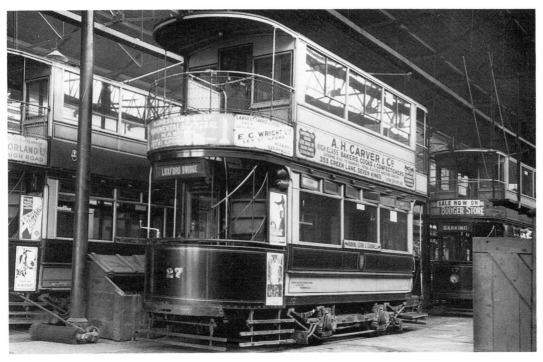

62.   Tram no. 27 at the depot. When Ilford's earliest covered car arrived for testing on 5 September 1903, it was the first such car in the London area. It was very primitive and locally acquired the name 'Noah's Ark' because of its shape.

63.   Looking down the entrance to the depot, apparently from the upper deck of a car. The first covered tram was found to cost more in electricity to run but this was more than compensated for by the takings, so covers were soon fitted to nine other cars, leaving only the end balconies open.

64. A policeman directs light traffic through the Broadway, while tram no. 33 prepares for the return journey to Barkingside. The system had soon settled down into two routes: Chadwell Heath to Barking (after Loxford, the route ran over Barking rails) and Ilford Broadway to Barkingside to the north.

65. A busy scene at the Broadway. In the early days, the manager of the Ilford tramways used a bicycle to travel around the system.

66. Two open-deckers pass in the High Road by the Broadway, as a woman with a pram dashes across the road. In spite of the occasional problems such as fires or the collapse of a lineside stanchion holding up the wires, Ilford's tramways proved uniquely successful.

67. This part of the Broadway was known as 'Cobweb Corner' because of the distinctive appearance of the tramwires. In the early days, the lines went in every direction, except north to south (the clock tower still stood in the way). An East Ham tram waits on Ilford Hill, on the Ilford side of the boundary, providing a service as far as Aldgate.

68.   The eastern terminus at Chadwell Heath. A quaint custom permitted by the management involved the tying of white ribbons to the front and rear handrails of the vehicles to signify a staff wedding – a black ribbon indicated a funeral.

69.   The southern boundary of the system at Loxford Bridge. At first people had to transfer to Barking vehicles at this point in their journey but later Ilford cars continued into Barking town. Unlike the trams in many other municipalities, the Ilford network made a good profit, with advertising on the cars adding to the revenue.

THE TRIANGLE, LOXFORD BRIDGE, ILFORD.

Tram Terminus, Barkingside.

70.   Tram no. 11 at Barkingside, the northern terminus, in the early years. *The Chequers Inn* on the left faces the police station in the background. A late evening postal collection by tram was arranged from here between 1925 and 1931. An oblong box painted red was hooked over the dashplate of the 9 p.m. weekday and 8.20 p.m. Sunday departures from the Broadway. Forty minutes later, on the tram's return to Ilford, the box was removed for emptying at the main post office.

71.   A fleet of no. 8 buses at their terminus outside the *Seven Kings Hotel* in 1911. In November 1908 the no. 8 was running from here to Shepherd's Bush daily. A competitor, the Great Eastern service, ran as far as Ilford Broadway. In 1909 the no. 8 was extended to West Kilburn (the *Falcon*) and in September 1910 to Willesden Green (the *Spotted Dog*), the destination shown here. On 20 June 1912, the no. 8 was withdrawn between the Bank and Seven Kings and the no. 25 to Victoria was substituted.

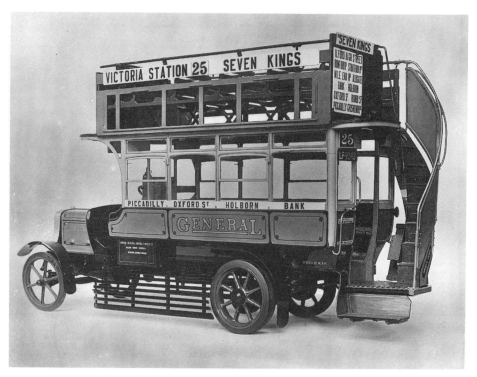

72. First introduced in 1910, the B-type bus was a standardised motor vehicle, a great improvement on its predecessors but still paying homage to the shape of the horse-bus. It was a very successful model, many hundreds proving themselves on the streets. A mainly hand-built bus, the wheels were fitted with solid rubber tyres which made the bus vibrate.

73. Seven Kings garage, the construction of which in 1913 consolidated the 'General' company's operations in this area, has replaced the private house and garden in the background of this shot. Two no. 25 buses are waiting in the hotel forecourt. The first is in Metropolitan livery. Metropolitan buses were operated by the L.G.O.C. under an agreement signed in October 1912 between the two companies. The hotel signboard has disappeared since the previous photograph was taken, although the nails can still be seen.

74. A typical bus company employee. Drivers and conductors were generally very dependable characters. Smart appearance and manner were encouraged by the larger companies.

75. An independent (Empress) bus at Gants Hill, Cranbrook Road. By the late 1920s the no. 26 route ran from Victoria station to Chigwell Row and the no. 26B from Victoria to Barkingside, both via Cranbrook Road. The arterial road roundabout can be seen behind the bus which is on a short working to Ilford station.

GENERAL

JUNE 1923

TOWN AND COUNTRY SERVICES BY LONDON'S MOTOR-BUSES.

ISSUED FREE

CHERTSEY BRIDGE

B 25 W'kdays
Service 8 mins
Fare 1/-

VICTORIA
Via Route 25 to Ilford thence via Cranbrook Rd
CRANBROOK PARK
BARKINGSIDE
Time 107 mins
Services : Cr'b'k Pk 8 mins
Barkingside 16 mins

B 25 Sundays
Service 10 mins.
Fare 1/2

VICTORIA
Via same as Weekday Route to Barkingside thence Fencepiece Rd, Grange Hill
CHIGWELL ROW
Time 110 mins.

26 Service W'kdays 60 mins Sundays 15 mins
Fare 1/2

STRATFORD
Via Forest Gate, Manor Pk, Ilford, Seven Kings, Goodmayes, Chadwell Heath, Romford, Gidea Park, Chelmsford Rd
BRENTWOOD
Time 85 mins

26 A Service W'kdays 60 mins Sundays 15 mins
Fare 10d.

STRATFORD
Via Route 26 to Romford thence via Hornchurch
UPMINSTER
Time 71 mins

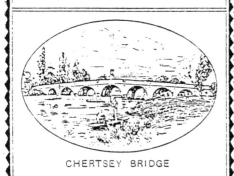

25 Service 4 mins
Fare 10d.

VICTORIA
Via Piccadilly, Bond St, Oxford St, Holborn, Bank, Aldgate, Mile End Road, Stratford Broadway, Romford Road
SEVEN KINGS
Time 97 mins

A 25 Service 8 mins
Fare 1/-

EBURY BRIDGE
Via Warwick St, Wilton Rd thence as Route 25 to Ilford thence Green Lane
BECONTREE HEATH (Three Travellers)
Time 114 mins

76. The General (L.G.O.C.) route list of 1923 shows the local services.

Electric City

Edwardian Ilford could already lay claim to the title Electric City. As soon as the town gained its freedom, it began to march firmly into the 20th century. Until the final years of the 19th century, gas had been the principal form of artificial lighting. It was supplied locally by the Ilford Gas Company which, by 1899, had been operating for 60 years. The new urban district was interested in purchasing this company but, having been rebuffed, it turned its attention to electricity generation. The idea had taken hold that electricity could be used for both lighting and transport. Events moved swiftly – the Ilford Act of Parliament was passed and a generating station was constructed in Ley Street. The installation of electricity began early in 1901. At the same time work was going ahead with the laying down of track for an electric tramway. The urban district lost no time in laying the basis of a model municipality. These new developments stimulated interest in modern shopping facilities which increased in line with the housing. Seven Kings, Goodmayes and Chadwell all had impressive local shopping terraces.

By the time the district was elevated to borough status in 1926, the municipal electric company was supplying the whole of its area, as well as certain premises at Chadwell Heath just over the border. The magnificent Town Hall, first opened in 1902 and extended on more than one occasion, joined the prosperous shops of the High Road in declaring Ilford's firm intention to make itself a success.

This pattern continued, although hindered somewhat by the First World War. By the 1920s there were many shops in the town paying homage to the new commercial god, electricity. Today the optimism of that age is still proclaimed by the lettering announcing 'Electric Parade' above shops in Seven Kings Road, opposite the railway station. 'Brilliant supplies' of 87 High Road had later managed to devise a name which gave just the right impression of up-to-dateness for an electrical goods and wireless (radio) suppliers. The wireless, gramophone and talking pictures became all the rage in the 1920s. In 1929, three local cinemas were listed in Kelly's Essex Directory: Seven Kings Cinema, 14 Cameron Road, Super Cinema and Café Lounge, Balfour Road (C & A's now occupies this site) and the Ilford Empire Kinema, Ilford Lane. Another cinema on the High Road, the Premier Electric Theatre (note the 'electric' in the name), had closed in 1925, but was replaced by the Ilford Palais de Danse of immortal fame. There was also the De Luxe Cinema standing in all its splendour in the midst of a line of shops at the Broadway end of the High Road.

Modern commercial enterprise was represented by several department stores, whose reputation stretched far beyond the town itself. These were Moultons, Wests, Harrison Gibsons and Bodgers. They attracted the shopping public from a wide area. Green's grocery stores supplied the bacon for a revival of the Dunmow Flitch ceremony in Ilford. From a small beginning in 1896, with a grocery and provision shop in the High Road, this company spread throughout Essex with 144 shops, 14 in the borough of Ilford. A food warehouse in the north of the borough supplied the chain.

Ilford's right to the title 'Electric City' had begun with the advent of the Council Tramways, providing fast and cheap local travel at the dawn of the Edwardian age. It reached its apex in the late 1930s with the arrival of the trolleybus, the tram's quiet successor gliding grandly through the shopping centres.

77.   All systems go in Ilford Lane in the 1930s. The trams will be departing in opposite directions.   Cyclists, pedestrians and a milk float mingle with the other vehicles. Behind the front tram, in the row of shops known as Broadway Market, is Giacinto Pinagli's dining rooms.

The Broadway, Ilford.

78. A busy scene in the Broadway, with newspaper sellers prominent. The photograph may have been taken on a Saturday, with men returning from a football match. The Super Cinema can be seen in the background.

79.   There is a notable absence of buses in this view of the Broadway looking east, between the two world wars.

The Broadway, Ilford.

80. The Ilford Gas Company advertises the advantages of its product, 1906. After 60 years of having the field to itself, it now had a strong competitor in the Urban District Electricity Department.

"ALL IN" 1^D. RATE
ONE PENNY
PER UNIT
FOR
ELECTRICITY
FOR LIGHTING, WATER-HEATING, COOKING, and ALL DOMESTIC PURPOSES.

(Providing an Electric Water Heater is installed).

1d. per Unit includes Supplying, Wiring, and Fixing an
ELECTRIC WATER HEATER

YOU PAY ONLY 5/- CONNECTING FEE

Ask for our representative to call.

BOROUGH OF ILFORD ELECTRICITY DEPARTMENT

Central Showrooms:
320-326, HIGH ROAD, ILFORD

Branch Showrooms:
525, GREEN LANE, GOODMAYES
HIGH ROAD, BARKINGSIDE

81. The battle was still raging in 1936 when this magazine advertisement stressed the reasonable connection fee for an electric water heater.

82. At the start of the Edwardian period, the High Road was already teaming with shops and people. In the background, Sainsbury's advertise butter.

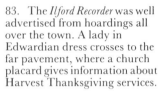

83. The *Ilford Recorder* was well advertised from hoardings all over the town. A lady in Edwardian dress crosses to the far pavement, where a church placard gives information about Harvest Thanksgiving services.

84. Looking in an opposite direction along the High Road, towards the Broadway. An amazing array of advertisements fills the corner wall of the undertakers on the left. Cyclists and horse-drawn vehicles are the main traffic.

Town Hall, Ilford

85.   Shops near the town hall included an old-style butcher's.

86.   An open-top tram makes its way towards Chadwell Heath via Seven Kings, though its rear indicator shows Barking. It has already passed Gibson's Jewellers and a man pulling a cart containing a piano. Vine church tower rises proudly in the background.

87. This is the fine shopping development that was built to serve the Downshall Estate. Conveniently placed next to Seven Kings station, it boasted an old-style Sainsbury's among the array of other shops.

88. A little further from the station, this corner drapery on half-day closing has a crowded window display typical of its period. The tram wires are now supported by poles at the side instead of in the middle of the road.

89. Meads Lane, a subsidiary shopping parade, contains much of interest, including the group outside Sinclair's and the shoe repairer in his window. Notice the name 'Eighteen' above one of the shops. The doorways seem far too narrow to accommodate any large numbers of customers.

90. This parade in the High Road, with accommodation above, is almost a standard pattern for a number of Ilford locations. There is a post and telegraph office, one of a great number set up at this time. On the far right one shop offers various beverages to catch the trade passing on the main street or on the way to or from the station just around the corner.

91.   On the other side of the railway, the Mayfield Estate, built by Cameron Corbett, M.P., was well served by this shopping development and Goodmayes station a short distance away.

92.   An elaborate elevation, still largely intact, graced these shops at Chadwell Heath, with the tram terminus and district boundary just beyond.

93. An enterprising Cranbrook Road business, 1906.

94.   A peaceful Edwardian view of Cranbrook Road.

95.   A later, more crowded view. Estate agents' offices face each other across the road in a suburb that is still growing.

GREATER LONDON'S
GREATEST FURNISHERS

Romance

STARTING in the High Road, Ilford, in 1902, when the surrounding neighbourhood was still rural, the firm of Harrison Gibson, Ltd., has grown with the town. Every year has seen an increase in the business which has generally been accompanied by enlargements to the premises.

The firm now occupies no less than 75,000 square feet of floor space, comprising the main Showrooms in the High Road, and the commanding building at the corner of Havelock Street and the large Furniture Depositories alongside the L.N.E. Railway.

In purchasing from us you are patronising your Local Furnishers, who, by employing over 130 people in this neighbourhood, contribute very substantially in wages and rates to the prosperity of the district.

HARRISON GIBSONS

The Ilford Furniture Store
Established 1902   HIGH ROAD. ILFORD

96. This view of Harrison Gibson's was used in advertisements of the late 1920s and early 1930s. Other advertisements extolled the 'variety, quality and beauty in furniture and home furnishings ... to be seen every day on our five Great Floors' and mentioned that browsers were not pestered to buy.

Telephone:
ILFORD · 0321 (2 LINES)

Telegrams:
HARRISON GIBSON · ILFORD

Bought of

HARRISON GIBSON LTD
ESTABLISHED 1902

HOUSE FURNISHERS

ILFORD
Essex

Mrs Mann
30 Nacton Lane
Hornchurch

IN YOUR REPLY PLEASE REFER TO 237

1929 192

Feb	18	yds Linoleum		5/9	5	3	6
	10½			5/11	3	2	1½
	10½			4/11	2	11	7½
	8½			4/6	1	18	3
	6½			4/6	1	9	3
	5			5/11	1	9	7
	8½		?	4/11	2	1	9
Opl	3	Ship mats		8/6	1	5	6
	14	O/S Grips		2/6	1	15	·
	4	Ends Bound		6		2	
	12½	yds Stair Carpet		11/6	7	3	9
		Laying ditto				3	6
	10	yds Linoleum Back Room		2/11½	1	9	7
	15	Stair Pads		5.		6	3
	3¼	yds Stair Carpet		11/6	1	17	4
	1	Rug			1	19	6
	2	Rev Rugs			1	19	10
		To Removal			2	5	
		To recovering chair in					
May		Tapestry			5	5	
1		B Fitting			1	11	6
				fwd fwd	19	11	

TERMS: NETT CASH

---

97. A customer's bill from 1929 shows the cost of setting up house in respect of lino, rugs, stair carpet etc. The total cost, carried forward onto a second sheet, was £54 16s. 4d. This included the further provision (presumably all for the bathroom) of a towel rail, toilet roll holder, hook, two tumblers, brush holder, 1½ yards of lino, underfelt and the major item, a 9 x 7 carpet at £6 15s.

WESTS
(ILFORD) LTD.

MILLINERY AND GOWNS.
GENERAL AND FANCY DRAPERY,
SOFT FURNISHING AND LINENS.

〰

DIRECTORS :
C. BARKER   W. H. WHITE
H. BAKER   H. WILLIS

Telephone - ILFORD 1141-1142

15, 17 & 19,
Cranbrook Road,

ILFORD 3rd February 193 4

Estimate to supply make and fix curtains and pelmet for ground floor front, and curtains and box pleated valance for 1st floor front. Complete with necessary fittings.

Ground floor front

	£	s	d
2 Curtains 2 widths each x 5'9½ o/a			
and 1 pelmet to shape braided only			
Using 10½ yards damask to be selected			
10½ yards lining at 1/11½ yard	1	0	7
1½ yards bump interlining 1/4½ yard		2	0½
10 yards braid at 8½ yard		7	1
4 yards buckram at 1/3		5	0
1 bay lath complete brackets	1	1	0
20'0 railway at 9d		15	0
Sundries		4	0
Making and fixing	2	2	6

£5 : 17 : 2½

Front bedroom

	£	s	d
2 Curtains 2 widths each x 4'9 o/a			
and 1 valance 6 widths x 11" o/a			
Using 9½ yards damask to be selected			
9½ yards lining at 1/11½ yard		18	7½
20'0 railway at 9d		15	0
11'0 valance rail at 6d		5	6
Sundries		4	0
Making and fixing	1	6	6

£3 : 9 : 7½

Summary

Ground floor front	*PLUS 10½ YDS* (damask to be selected)	£5 : 17 : 2½
Front Bedroom	*PLUS 9½ YDS* (damask to be selected)	£3 : 9 : 7½

98. Five years later, in 1934, our Hornchurch housewife is still coming back to do her shopping in Ilford. This time she chooses Wests to supply, make and fix curtains. The total cost, with the fixing, is £13 6s. ½d.

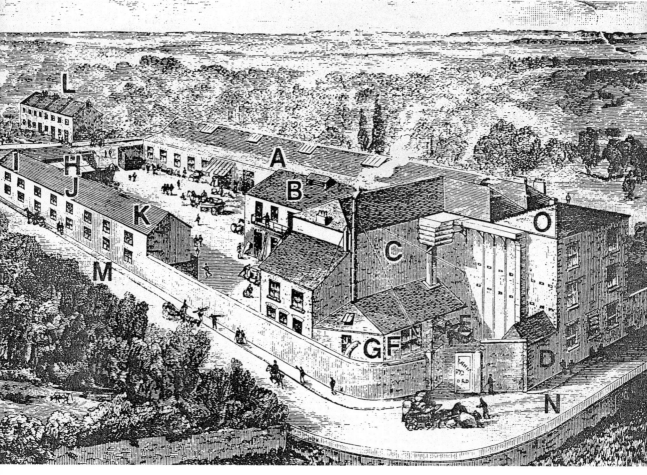

99.   An engraving of the Britannia Works, 1888. Alfred Harman founded this company in the town to make photographic dry plates. This view is distorted to underline the factory's rural situation on the banks of the Roding with Uphall beyond. The key is as follows: A = coating rooms; B = printing out paper stores; C = P.O.P. emulsion & cutting; D = covered passage with ice-well beneath; F = engine room; J = glass drying; K = glass examining; N = Grove Terrace (which later became Uphall Road).

100. A view of the Britannia Works from the west in 1895. The track from left to right became Uphall Road. Houses were later built on the cabbage patch.

101. Workers outside the Ilford premises.

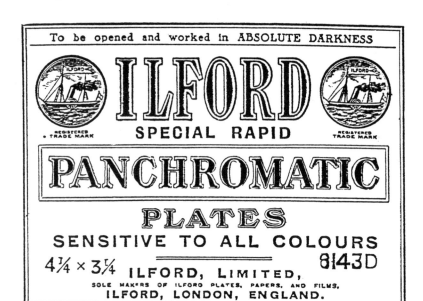

102a. & b. Labels from an unopened packet of glass plates. The small label indicates that this packet was destined for the Far East and reminds us that the market for Ilford photographic products was worldwide.

103. Much thought was put into packaging and advertising – an example of the varied designs on film wallets between the two world wars.

104. On Charter Day, 21 October 1926, the Duke and Duchess of York came to Ilford for the presentation. For one event they came to the Super Cinema (where C & A now stands) and their visit drew the crowds. All traffic, including a no. 26 double-decker bus, was halted while they were in the building. Ilford's new borough status confirmed that it had 'arrived' in the big league of British towns.

105. Trolley wires at the Chequers Corner sum up Ilford's strong connection with electric transport.

106. Wintry morning in Ley Street but the reliable trolleybus is there to transport passengers to work or the shops. Note the three white bands round the trolley poles for visibility.

Fire, Flood & Commotion

In the mid-19th century, most fires in Ilford were those in haystacks, necessitating the use of fire-hooks. This was just as well as the only fire appliances which the town could call upon in 1871 were a few lengths of leather hose carried to fires in a wheelbarrow. Fortunately, the situation began to improve soon afterwards. For instance, in 1884, a fire-escape ladder was bought for the town by the Lighting Inspectors. The equipment available for fighting fires was housed at the *Red Lion* public house on Ilford Hill. Tasker said the hose was still in use in 1901 and bore the letters 'I. W.' (standing for the Ilford Ward of Barking). In 1890, a volunteer fire brigade was eventually created. Four years later, a fire station with a caretaker's house was built in Oakfield Road and a steam fire engine was acquired. Out-stations with hose-carts were at Barkingside (1897), Seven Kings (1899) and Horns Village (near the public house of that name, 1901). The local fire brigade began to acquire kudos under a charismatic chief officer, John Woollard. They also won the All-England Fire Escape Challenge Shield two years in succession (1898-9). In a comparatively short time, owing to Ilford's growth, a bigger central fire station was required and this was situated in Ley Street, opening in 1905. The first motor fire-engine was purchased in 1914.

In 1924, a large fire occurred in the centre of the town. John Harrison Gibson, the founder of the big store of that name, had recently died and his son had only just taken charge when fire broke out at the store. Apparently, a man on a passing tram noticed smoke coming from one of the windows, at 8 a.m. He jumped off the tram to give the alarm but the flames, caused by a fault in the electrical wiring, had already spread and one whole side of the 150-foot frontage was an inferno. The rest of the building succumbed quite quickly. The splendid stock – carpets, curtains and furniture – burnt fiercely amidst smoke and flames; the huge plate glass windows shattered and the floors crashed down in the ruins. The firemen fought bravely but, in this case, were unequal to the task.

Over the centuries, Ilford has had to cope with the problem of flooding, when the River Roding overflowed its banks. An ancient tale recounts that when St Ethelwald, Bishop of Essex, died at Barking Abbey, his corpse was carried to Ilford where the river was in flood. A miracle allowed the flood to abate while the funeral procession passed over the waters and later along the Great Road to London; a flood on the River Lea was similarly negotiated. In the Middle Ages, the bridges at Ilford were often broken down and in disrepair due to the flood waters. Sometimes, however, more severe floods occurred, as in 1888 when Ilford, Romford and Chelmsford suffered seriously from the results of a prolonged bout of torrential rain. Only 15 years later, Ilford was surprised by another flood following three days of continuous downpour. On 15 June 1903, the river began rising in the morning and livestock were evacuated from the water meadows to higher ground. It was not long before water had covered the riverside fields between Wanstead Park and Ilford and, by early evening, the scene resembled a view across the sea. The waters advanced quietly and stealthily. Here and there, a wall collapsed beneath the waves but, apart from the sound of the rain, only the sighing and trickling of flowing water could be heard. As the evening progressed, the full horror of the flood could be appreciated, as the water began to fill the back gardens of houses in Wanstead Park Road. Commuters living in the Cranbrook Park neighbourhood returned from the city only to discover, in amazement, that they had to wade through the water to reach their homes. In most houses, water had reached the lower stairs and the ground floor was no longer habitable. The Seven Kings Brook also overflowed and the tramway was flooded as far as the *Seven Kings Hotel*. The railway track resembled a wide, shallow river. Meanwhile, the

107. (*above*) The new fire station, Ley Street, photographed from the open ground opposite.

108. (*right*) Ilford's fire chief, John Woollard, produced this postcard himself, listing the posts he held. He often sent it as a Christmas card to local dignitaries.

109. (*left*) Not one of Ilford's fire engines, but typical of the neighbouring machines which might have been called upon to help with bigger blazes.

110. (*below*) Only the trees and parts of collapsed dividing walls show above the water in these back gardens, during the 1903 flood.

Roding carried all kinds of debris such as small trees, wooden household items, furniture and boxes on its rapid tide. Rafts, made out of anything which came to hand, were soon employed in desperate salvage efforts. The built-up streets of Manor Park on the other side of the river were also badly affected. Fortunately, the rain stopped on Monday night, avoiding further disaster. Ilford gradually returned to normal but those who experienced the events of that day never forgot them.

On New Year's Day 1915 there was a serious train accident at Ilford. The early Clacton to London train ran into a local train from Gidea Park. The express was travelling at 50 m.p.h. and the driver 'misread one signal for another near the scene of the accident', thus concluding that the line was clear whereas in fact the signal was registering danger. Ten people were killed and approximately thirty were seriously injured. The injured were nearly all residents of Seven Kings, as was one lady, Miss Bertha Christie, who was killed. The passengers on the Clacton train were not seriously injured. The inquest revealed that the loss of life would have been much worse but for the presence of mind of the Gidea Park train guard who was specially commended by the jury for his prompt application of the brakes, thus 'saving the lives of hundreds of other passengers' in the rear section of the local train. The inquest jury also expressed the opinion that all guard's vans should have rear-view lookouts attached to the back of the train. It was stated that the number of trains passing through Ilford station between 8 a.m. and 10 a.m. was 72, or approximately one every two minutes. All the emergency services combined to help the injured.

At the turn of the century, respectable Ilford witnessed a series of dramatic scenes. The first of these incidents began at 10 p.m. on 18 May 1900, when news of the Relief of Mafeking reached Britain. The siren of Ilford Paper Mill echoed over the town for ten minutes. At once, a large gathering of people swarmed towards Ilford Broadway. Coloured flares and fireworks were discharged and patriotic singing began. One individual marched up and down tolling an enormous handbell. Musicians formed themselves into a band, playing popular tunes in front of the *Angel Inn*. At this point, two large horses harnessed to a heavy wagon took fright and ran wildly down the High Road. There were no casualties and the horses were finally stopped at the Broadway. By 3 a.m., the public uproar had subsided.

A few weeks later, when the Boer capital of Pretoria was captured, the celebrations grew wilder. The people of Ilford, relieved of the heavy strain of bad news, were now determined to make it a night to remember. Possibly, too much alcohol was consumed and dangerous bonfires were started in many streets. The police were not sure how to proceed and, while one contingent was preventing any more kindling being added to one blaze in a side street, another huge pyre was lit in the middle of the Broadway. The flames were clearly visible above the rooftops. By now, tightly-packed crowds jammed the Broadway, stopping the police from approaching in force. More kindling material was passed above people's heads including cartloads of builders' timber, and shutters dismantled from shopfronts. A large hoarding which guarded Bodger's new premises was completely stripped. In desperation, the fire brigade was called out once more, but they were unequal to the task and soon had to retire. In the scuffles, the fire engine was almost overturned, equipment was badly damaged and the hoses were slashed. The scene gradually quietened down and, by 2 a.m., most people had returned home.

The next evening, however, the crowd began to form again, starting a new bonfire in the Broadway on the ashes of the old fire. One mounted policeman had prevented a pile of timber scaffolding and floor-boards being removed from Clements Road. Elsewhere,

111. A view over the 'lake'. Boundaries between properties disappeared.

over-reaction on the part of the police brought in heavy-handed reinforcements from outside Ilford. Worried by their inability to prevent the build-up of crowds, police chiefs brought in mounted police to charge every large group of celebrators. Many innocent people were caught up in the confusion. Broadway soon resembled a battlefield, with many onlookers injured by police truncheons. The victims included a lamplighter trying to finish his round, who later regained consciousness in the Salisbury House surgery of Dr. James Shimeld, a famous Ilford personality. The crowds were finally broken up but there had been unnecessary brutality for which the police were later reprimanded.

Fortunately, when news of the end of the Boer War was received, the police were able to handle festivities with more circumspection. On the following Monday, flags were everywhere and even the dogs were decorated in red, white and blue. In the evening, polite official celebrations were ignored by many, who preferred to light the customary street fires. However, a police cordon ensured that the fire in the Broadway was kept within bounds, preventing the addition of further fuel. A smaller bonfire on wasteland opposite the *Coach and Horses* was allowed to burn itself out, but not before 50 wooden barrels had been consumed in the flames.

112. More of the havoc which affected a huge area on both sides of the Roding.

113. Another of local photographer Watson Hornby's pictures showing a horse and cart pausing at the corner of Empress Avenue and Wanstead Park Road which are both covered by water.

114. The women of the neighbourhood inspect the flood damage.

115. Slow progress by horse and cart along what is now almost a canal.

ILFORD MURDER MYSTERY.

WIFE AND YOUTH ARRESTED.

The murder early on Wednesday morning of a City clerk named Percy Thompson, while he was returning home with his wife along Belgrave-road, Ilford, is surrounded by mystery, and the circumstances are being closely investigated by Scotland Yard detectives.

The victim of the outrage, a man of slight build, aged 33, was in the employ of a City shipping firm, with whom he had been for 12 years. He lived with his wife, whom he married about six years ago, at The Retreat, 41, Kensington-gardens. It appears that at about 12.30 a.m. Mr. Thompson and his wife, returning home from a theatre, were walking along Belgrave-road, and when within a hundred yards of their residence the man was suddenly and savagely attacked. He was stabbed a number of times about the neck and head, apparently with a pair of scissors, and died within a few minutes. His injuries were of a shocking character, among them being the severance of the jugular artery. The screams of his wife attracted the attention of two passers-by, who rushed forward to assist. A doctor was hastily sent for, but on his arrival at the scene of the crime he saw at once that the man was dead, and ordered the removal of the body to the mortuary.

Mrs. Thompson, in a very hysterical state, was taken home, and later in the day was visited by the police. She went to the police station, and was asked to give what details she could of the affair. The wife, it is understood, was engaged at a millinery shop in the City, and it was the custom of Mr. and Mrs. Thompson, who seemed to live on happy terms, to go to the City together each morning, and often meet and return home by the same train at night. They were regarded as being fairly comfortable, and about two years ago purchased the house in which they were living at Kensington-gardens.

The crime presents baffling features, as apparently nobody has come forward who saw the assailant, and an all-day search in the roadway and gardens of Belgrave-road and Kensington-gardens failed to trace the weapon with which the crime was committed.

There was a dramatic development on Thursday, when Edith Thompson, the wife of the deceased man; and Frederick Bywaters, 20, a ship's steward, of Westow-street, Upper Norwood, S.E., were arrested on suspicion of being concerned in the murder of the woman's husband.

116 & 117. Early developments in the Bywaters/Thompson murder case. Mrs. Edith Thompson and her boyfriend Frederick Bywaters (pictured here) were later found guilty of the murder and hanged. Many afterwards felt that the sentence on Edith Thompson was a judgement on her morals rather than on her true guilt in the affair.

The inquest on the body of the victim was opened at Ilford Town Hall on Friday morning by Dr. Ambrose.

The Coroner, at the outset, said it would be necessary to adjourn the inquiry to allow the police to complete their inquiries.

William Eustace Graydon, 231, Shakespeare-crescent, Manor Park, said he had identified the body of the deceased as that of Percy Thompson, who was his son-in-law, aged 32.

The Coroner intimated that this was as far as they could proceed at present; and the inquiry was adjourned until Thursday, October 19th, at 10 o'clock.

A DAGGER FOUND.

Ever since the murder the police have been searching for the weapon with which the deed might have been committed, and on Monday they found a dagger in a drain in Seymour-gardens, about five minutes walk from the scene of the murder. The dagger has a double-edged blade about 5½in. long, and a black chequered pattern handle about 4in. long.

ACCUSED AT COURT.

Some time before the opening of the Court a queue of people, principally men, assembled outside in the hope of securing admission. Only a few of the general public were allowed in.

The female prisoner, who is 28 years of age, is a slightly-built woman. Of very youthful and prepossessing appearance, she seemed ill and nervous, and was supported by the police matron. She wore a brown cloth coat with big fur collar, and on entering the dock she turned the collar up and completely hid her face. She was given a seat in the dock, and her hat was removed.

The male prisoner, a youth of respectable appearance, was quite composed. A detective stood between the two prisoners, who had been brought to the Court in separate conveyances.

Det.-inspr. Hall stated that on Thursday morning he saw Mrs. Thompson at 41, Kensington-gardens, Ilford, and said to her " I am an inspector of police. I understand you were with your husband early this morning in Belgrave-road. I am satisfied that he was assaulted and stabbed several times." She replied " We were coming along Belgrave-road, and just past the corner of Kensington-gardens I heard him call out ' Oh! ' and he fell up against me. I put out my arms to save him, and found blood, which I thought was coming from his mouth. I tried to help him up, but he staggered for several yards against Kensington-gardens. He then fell against the wall and slid down. He did not speak to me. I cannot say if I spoke to him. I felt his clothing wet with blood. He never moved after he fell. We had no quarrel on the way. We were quite happy together. Immediately I saw the blood I ran across the road to a doctor's. I appealed to a lady and gentleman who were passing, and the gentleman also went to the doctor's. The doctor came and told me my husband was dead. Just before he fell down I was walking on his right-hand side, on the inside of the pavement nearest the wall. We were side by side. I did not see anybody about at the time. My husband and I were talking about going to a dance " Witness added that the woman subsequently made other statements, but he was not prepared to put those in at the moment.

The Clerk. Was she very agitated?—She appeared to be.

Continuing, witness said that at 7 p.m. he saw the male prisoner at Ilford Police Station. He made a statement, which witness did not propose to put in yet, and witness took possession of his overcoat.

On this evidence prisoners were remanded till Wednesday.

We are informed that since the case was heard Mr. F. A. S. Stern has been instructed to appear for Mrs. Thompson.

* The founder was a Mr. Daniel Day, a block and pump maker, at Wapping: he used to invite a select party of his friends to feast on beans and bacon, under the shade of the oak. In the course of a few years, other parties were formed on Mr. Day's anniversary; these increasing, booths were erected, and various articles brought for sale: about the year 1725, it became a regular fair. For several years prior to the decease of Mr. Day, the pump and block makers of Wapping, to the number of 30 or 40, went to the fair in a boat made of one entire piece of fir, mounted on a coach carriage, drawn by six horses, adorned with flags and streamers, attended by a band of music and a number of persons on horseback and foot; and a few years before his death, his favourite tree lost a large branch, out of which he procured a coffin to be made for his own interment. He died October 19, 1767, aged 84: his remains were conveyed by water to Barking, according to his own request, (for, having been thrown from a horse, and overturned in a wheel carriage, he conceived an antipathy to both,) accompanied by six journeymen block and pump makers, to each of whom he bequeathed a new leather apron and a guinea. In June, 1805, this tree received great damage from fire, either by a party who had been regaling under its branches, or from gypsies; it was discovered by the sparks to be on fire, and was with difficulty extinguished: the main branch on the south side, with part of the body, was consumed, and it has decayed very rapidly since. On the fair-day of 1813, a gentleman gave a boy half a crown to procure for him the last green sprig off the end of one of the branches; and when the drawing was made for the vignette, in the August following, there was not a leaf on it.

118. Fairlop Fair, the origin of which has already been recorded, did become rather a rowdy event. These high jinks accelerated the demise of the great oak; fires lit in the base of the trunk finally killed it. The original land was also closed off to the revellers but the fair continued at nearby sites with various degrees of success throughout the 19th century. The voyage of the Fairlop Boats stopped at the beginning of this century.

Education, Health & Recreation

119. A class at Christchurch Road school in its early days. The variety of necklines illustrates how mothers handled the problem of dressing a child for school.

120. The Ursuline High School for Girls was set up in 1903. The sender of this postcard commented, 'This is where we have "Degrees" on Fridays'. Notice the multiple use of the hall as assembly hall, art room and theatre.

ESTABLISHED 1894.

MULLEY'S SCHOOL

— for —

Shorthand, Typewriting, Bookkeeping, French, German, and Handwriting,

— **6,** —

CLEVELAND RD., ILFORD.

Ilford, 21st September, 1908.
Mr. MULLEY,
Ilford School of Shorthand,
Cleveland Road.
Dear Sir.—Allow me to thank you for the attention and instruction you have given my son in Shorthand and Typewriting during the time he has been attending your classes, also for the situation you were kind enough to find him with Mr. where, after a week's trial, he has given satisfaction and is retained.—Yours sincerely,

Ilford, 4th December, 1908.
E. W. MULLEY, Esq.,
Cleveland Road, Ilford.
Dear Sir.—I must apologise for not writing to you before in order to thank you for obtaining a situation for my daughter, with which she is very well satisfied. I must also congratulate you for so successful an achievement in making her efficient in less than five months. I shall, without hesitation, gladly recommend anyone desiring a similar training to undertake a course of study under your system.—Faithfully yours,

Open daily from 9 a.m. to 10 p.m. | *Telephone 858 Ilford.* | *Please call or write for Prospectus.*

121. E. W. Mulley's Commercial Academy must have given many candidates the edge in job applications by providing them with extra skills.

122.   The Park Higher Grade school, Melbourne Road, was taken over by the County Council from Ilford School Board in 1904. It had been one of the first of its kind in Essex. The buildings shown here were occupied in 1935 after the girls had transferred to their separate school in Cranbrook Road (1929).

123.   Cranbrook College for Boys started in Cranbrook Lodge in 1896.

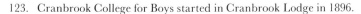

124. Claybury, one of two large mental institutions with extensive grounds, was opened in the Borough by outside bodies. It was the first lunatic asylum of its kind to be erected by the London County Council and was opened in 1893 in the grounds of the old mansion of the same name which was also pressed into use as an annexe.

125. Claybury was said to be one of the most modern and up-to-date institutions of its kind when built, as this photograph of the hall testifies.

126.   The staff cricket team at the West Ham Borough Asylum, Goodmayes. The man in the middle of the second row is the chief officer and the man in ordinary clothes, the steward. The building of the asylum began in 1899, taking two years to complete. The grounds covered 110 acres.

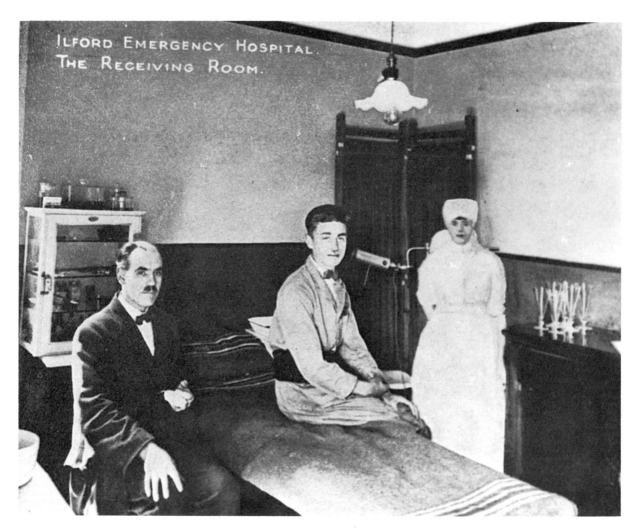

127. The Receiving Room of the Ilford Emergency Hospital. Opened in 1912, it was later rebuilt on the same site and became the King George V Hospital, Eastern Avenue, opened in 1930.

128.   New forms of treatment, including the use of electrical apparatus, were adopted at the Ilford Emergency Hospital. This photograph shows the Massage Room.

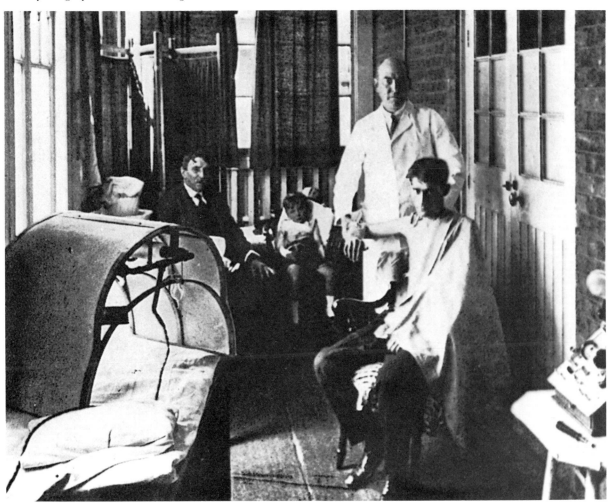

129. A view from the forecourt of the hospital. There was also an Isolation Hospital in Chadwell Heath Lane, opened in 1900.

130. A ceremony of blessing the ambulance, for use in the First World War.

131. Children pose by the rustic fences and unique clocktower in Cranbrook Park. This was originally called Central Park and later became Valentines Park.

132. The lakeside and boathouse.

133.   Boats on the lake.

134.   Ladies enjoying a sedate promenade near the water lilies.

PRUDENTIAL SEVEN KINGS SECTION.

Reading from left to right :—Messrs. P. J. Peacock, S. T. Hollis, E. J. Ealden, W. Morcombe, F. C. Cogswell (assistant). H. E. Anderson, A. J. Nunn, A. E. W. Sooley, A. J. Baldwin.

135.   Prudential Seven Kings Cycling Section.

136.   Ilford Cricket Club, *c.*1930.

137.   Hazeldene Boys Football Club team photograph.

138.   The Dunmow Flitch Ceremony was revived both in its birthplace (Dunmow) and at Ilford. The caption to the picture states that the winner is Fred Groves, M.P., probably an error for T. E. Groves, Labour M.P. for Stratford between the wars.

139. A jolly social event, possibly a Sunday School celebration, is held in full view of the street.

140. The surprised winner of the Beauty Contest receives applause at Ilford's Whit Monday Fête, 1912.

Mr. ANDREW BLACK. Miss BERTHA BIRD. Mr. ANDERSON NICOL.

SOUVENIR of Miss BERTHA BIRD'S Grand <u>OVERFLOW</u> Concert, at Ilford, 11th Nov. 1903.

141. The rear of this card, dated 1903, is typed with the invitation: 'I hope you are coming to Miss Bertha Bird's Grand Overflow Concert in Ilford Town Hall on Wednesday next 11th Nov. It will be a most ex-cellent concert and you are sure of spending an enjoyable evening. Yours sincerely, Jno. Ferguson. Concert Secretary'. The card is addressed in ink to Miss L. S. E. Greenfield, 87 Kensington Gardens.

142.   The flags are out on the Broadway in 1905, perhaps a Bank Holiday Fête.

143.   A slightly unattractive side view of the Hippodrome Theatre. The Mills Bros. are appearing on a typical programme. Passengers are climbing aboard a tram whilst the trolley pole is adjusted for the return journey to Barkingside.

144. On the right hand side of this view is the Hippodrome Theatre, opened in 1909. It was later used as a music hall and films were also shown here. The theatre was part of a redevelopment of Ilford Lane, when the corner was taken back to allow more room for traffic.

145. A view east along the High Road from just beyond the Broadway shows the De-Luxe Cinema, constructed from two shop units and opened in 1911. On the left are Boot's Cash Chemists and Lipton's. Singer Sewing Machines are at no. 94, on the right, just before the cinema.

146. The Premier Electric Theatre stood on the site later taken over by the famous Ilford Palais de Danse. Matinees are advertised at 3 o'clock. The building resembles some of the Carnegie Libraries of the Edwardian era.

147.   Crowds in front of the Ilford Super Cinema, on the corner of Ley Street and Cranbrook Road, on 21 October 1926. They are gathered to watch the Duke and Duchess of York take part in a Charter Day event inside the cinema.

148. A party of men are off to the pub at the *Cauliflower*. Huggins Fine Ales is the brew on offer at this hotel. It looks as if only one tram track is in operation at this time.

149. A wagonette setting off on an outing from the *White Horse*, at the beginning of the century. Many pleasant rural destinations could be reached in a comparatively short journey.

The White Horse Hotel,
BROADWAY, ILFORD.
Proprietor - W. D. GOLDING.

LUNCHEONS, DINNERS, & TEAS PROVIDED.

BILLIARDS—POOL & PYRAMIDS

TWO TABLES.

Wines, Spirits, and Beers of the Best Quality.

Head-Quarters of the Ilford Football Club, and Caterer to
the Ilford Sports Company.

ANGEL HOTEL, ILFORD
Proprietor, H. CHOWN.

THE SALOON AND OTHER CAPACIOUS BARS

NOW OPEN FOR BUSINESS.

Chops, Steaks, and Teas Supplied on Shortest Notice.

Billiard Saloon Now Open.

Wines and Spirits of the Finest Quality.

Wholesale and Retail.

THE COACH AND HORSES, ROMFORD ROAD, ILFORD

ACCOMMODATION FOR SMOKING CONCERTS.

QUOIT GROUND.

WINES AND SPIRITS OF THE FINEST QUALITY

Proprietor : J. H. GRAHAM.

150a. & b. Six Ilford hostelries vie for the reader's custom in a newspaper of 1899.

151. Whalebone House at Chadwell Heath. The whalebones over the entrance gate are shaded by the trees.

152. A summer Sunday at Red Bridge in 1905. The bridge, like many of the Roding crossings, was a rather narrow joining point between two parishes. Half of it was in Ilford parish and half in Wanstead. By 1900 concern was expressed that the bridge, which had last been rebuilt in 1840, was no longer capable of carrying the heavier traffic going over it.

153.   The Barnado Girls' Homes at Barkingside. As a student training at London Hospital, Barnardo stumbled on the dreadful conditions in which destitute children lived. His first home was only for boys. When he conceived the idea of housing girls in 'family' groups in separate cottages, the land at Barkingside provided an ideal location.

154.   The Cairns Memorial Cottage and clock tower with the children's church in the girls' village. Barnardo had opened a home for girls at Mossford Lodge in 1873; the girls' village followed in 1876.

155. Queen Victoria House. When first opened, the village consisted of 25 cottages. Although Barnardo received over £3,250,000 to carry on his work during his lifetime, he died owing nearly £50,000. A fund set up in his memory soon cleared the debt.

156. A general view of the grounds of the model village. A boys' village was founded nearby, but beyond the Ilford boundary, at Woodford Bridge. On the back of the postcards sold in aid of the Barnardo enterprise it was stated that his 'family' was the largest in the world – 7,300 children. Altogether, 98,000 had been admitted over the years.

157. Doctor Barnardo celebrating his birthday for the last time at Barkingside – he was to die shortly after this 60th anniversary, exhausted from overwork. In one month, he received 27,390 letters and, with the help of his staff, replied to nearly all of them.

158. The funeral procession leaving Barkingside railway station, mourned by his loyal hand-picked staff and the children (many of whom were now grown-up) he had worked most of his life to protect.

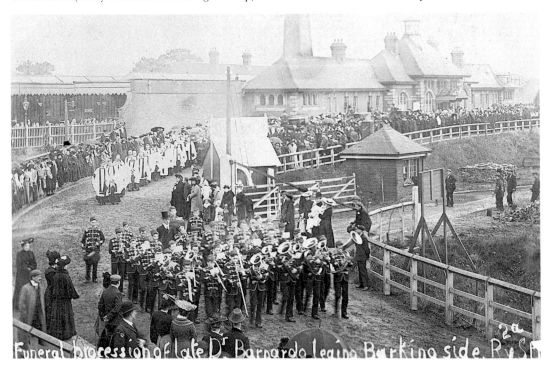

Funeral procession of late D�r Barnardo leaing Barking side Ry St.

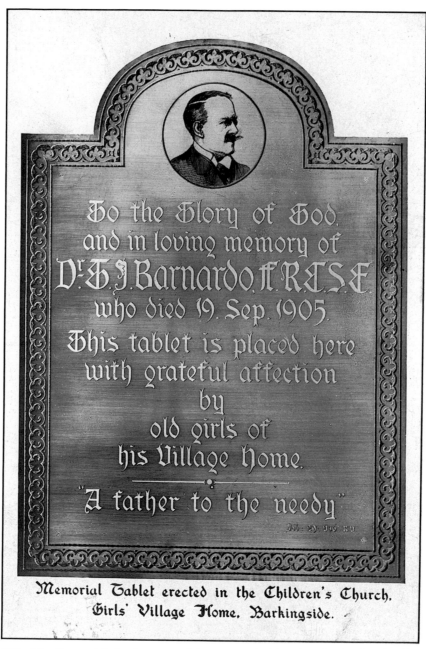

To the Glory of God,
and in loving memory of
Dr. T. J. Barnardo, F.R.C.S.E.
who died 19. Sep. 1905
This tablet is placed here
with grateful affection
by
old girls of
his Village Home.

"A father to the needy"

Job 29: 16 RV

Memorial Tablet erected in the Children's Church.
Girls' Village Home. Barkingside.

159. After Barnardo's death, a memorial was erected with an inscribed tablet, the gift of old girls of the village home. The best epitaph were the words spoken by a mourner, 'Earth is poorer, Heaven is richer'. He had always been especially interested in the very ill and the handicapped among his children. Another Ilford connection with Barnado was the Home for Cripples which he founded, known as the Children's Fold.

The Ilford Carnivals

160. South Hainault banner waits in front, ready to lead this section in the eagerly-awaited event of the year, the Ilford Hospital Carnival.

161. Park Ward at the bottom of Cranbrook Road. Several of these shops were to change hands over the next few years. This is probably the 1905 carnival.

162. A group of musicians in the schoolyard, with children looking on.

163. A bevy of beauties from North Hainault are the stars of the 1912 carnival. The competition between the floats from various wards was intense, contributing to neighbourhood spirit and Ilford's overall community strength.

ILFORD CARNIVAL. JULY. 1912

164.   A cargo of strange creatures ready to set off from a side road.

165.   Judging by the faces and the flags, a good day is about to begin as the procession prepares to move off outside Aldborough Road schools.

166. The queen of the soap bubbles receives the applause of the crowd in the July 1910 carnival.

167. These two confident young men from Sainsbury's appeared in the 1914 carnival with a very attractive tricycle float, just before the outbreak of the First World War.

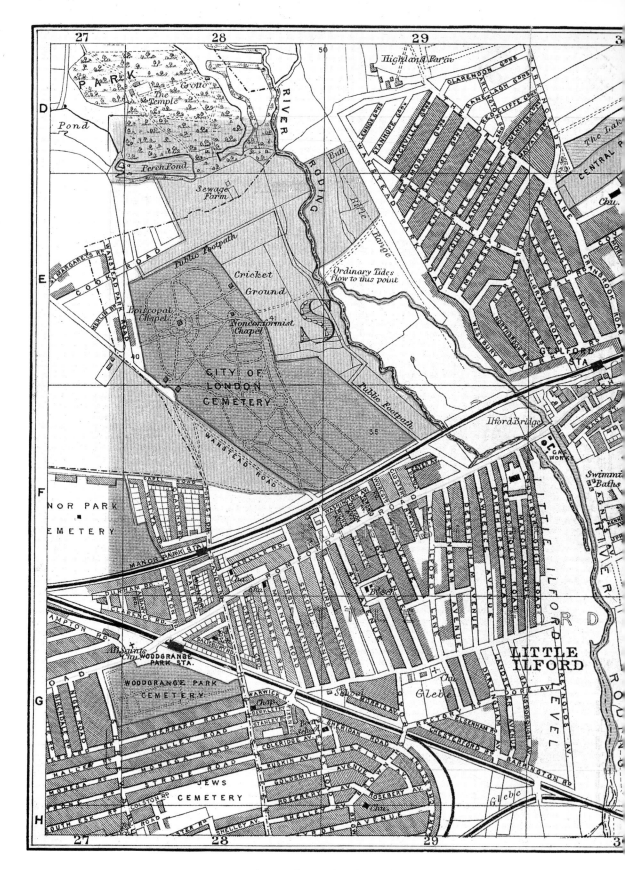

Street plan of Ilford pre-1914.